CW00539019

Text: *Keith Fergus*
Series editor: *Tony Bowerman*
Photographs: *Keith Fergus/ www. scottishhorizons.photoshelter.com, Paul Saunders Photography/www.paulsaundersphotography.com, Jon Douglas/www.flickr.com/jondouglas, Tony Bowerman, iStock/Getty Images, Shutterstock, Dreamstime, Wikipedia Commons*

Design: *Carl Rogers*

Northern Eye Books

ISBN 978-1-908632-43-2

A CIP catalogue record for this book is available from the British Library.

Cover: *Loch Katrine from the summit of Ben A'an (Walk 8)*
Photo: *Jon Douglas/ www.flickr.com/jondouglas*

Important Advice: The routes described in this book are undertaken at the reader's own risk. Walkers should take into account their level of fitness, wear suitable footwear and clothing, and carry food and water. It is also advisable to take the relevant OS map with you in case you get lost and leave the area covered by our maps.

Whilst every care has been taken to ensure the accuracy of the route directions, the publishers cannot accept responsibility for errors or omissions, or for changes in the details given. Nor can the publisher and copyright owners accept responsibility for any consequences arising from the use of this book.

If you find any inaccuracies in either the text or maps, please write or email us at the address below. Thank you.

This edition published in 2016 by
Northern Eye Books Limited
Northern Eye Books, Tattenhall, Cheshire CH3 9P
Email: tony@northerneyebooks.com
For sales enquiries, please call 01928 723 744

www.northerneyebooks.co.uk
www.top10walks.co.uk

Twitter: @outdoorfergie
@Northerneyeboo
@Top10walks

Contents

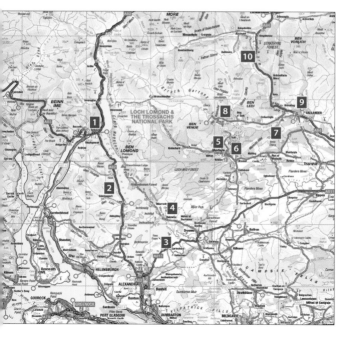

Scotland's first National Park

IN 2002 LOCH LOMOND AND THE TROSSACHS became Scotland's first National Park (the Cairngorms became Scotland second, and so far only other National Park, a year later).

It covers an area of 720 square miles and boasts 40 mountains over 2,500 feet in height including some of Scotland's most iconic Munro's and Corbett's: Ben Lomond, the craggy peaks of Ben Vorlich and Stuc a Chroin above Loch Earn, big, brutish and beautiful mountains like Ben Lui, Stob Binnien and Cruach Ardrain and the incomparable Ben Arthur (better known as The Cobbler), to name but a few.

Also within the National Park's confines are around 50 rivers and burns, 3 National Nature Reserves, 2 Forest Parks and 22 large lochs (plus numerous smaller lochs and lochans), including Loch Lomond, Loch Katrine and Loch Venachar, a of which hosts to a huge array of wildlife.

This breathtaking scenery and wildlife attracts approximate 4 million visitors each year.

Loch Lomond and its many islands from Ben Lomond

Easy Summits

The Loch Lomond and the Trossachs National Park straddles the Highland Boundary Fault Line and consequently has a magnificent array of rugged mountains, many rising to over 3,000 feet above sea level.

However, the park is also home to numerous lower peaks, which still offer a challenge but are within reach of the general walker. The views are just as astounding as those from their bigger cousins.

These easier summits provide a good introduction for those less experienced (including children) to the wonderful pursuit of hillwalking.

"Loch Lomond, the last, the most beautiful of the Caledonian lakes. The first view of it from Tarbat presents an extensive serpentine winding amidst lofty hills"

Thomas Pennant, *A Tour in Scotland*, 1769

TOP 10 **Walks:** Hill Walks & Easy Summits

The ten walks described here are accessible from villages such as Luss, Aberfoyle and Balmaha and are an ideal way to explore the high ground of Loch Lomond and The Trossachs National Park. Ben A'an, Duncryne and Conic Hill are forever popular while the more rugged terrain of Beinn Dubh, Beinn an t-Sidhein and Cruach Tairbeirt offer a certain sense of wildness.

But whichever route you choose, a fabulous walk is guaranteed amid some incredible scenery.

Cruach Tairbeirt — page 8

Beinn Dubh & Mid Hill — page 1

Duncryne — page 20

Conic Hill — page

The long finger-like Loch Lomond viewed from Cruach Tairbeirt

Cruach Tairbeirt

It's said that smaller hills grant the best views — and Cruach Tairbeirt's wonderful views certainly back this up

What to expect:
Good paths through forest with one boggy section. Steep, grassy hillside above the treeline

Distance/time: 8 kilometres/ 5 miles. Allow 3½ hours

Ascent/Descent: 405 metres/1,328 feet

Start: The large car park in Tarbet. Parking is free but it can get very busy, particularly during the summer months. Alternative parking is limited within the village

Grid ref: NN 320 045

Ordnance Survey Map: Explorer OL 38 Loch Lomond *South Dumbarton & Helensburgh Drymen & Cove*

After the walk: Restaurant/café/hotel in Tarbet

Walk outline

A climb onto Cruach Tairbeirt is a walk of 'two halves'. Initially, an excellent loop path strikes through woodland but once left behind a short, very boggy section continues. After crossing a burn, a firm path leads onto open hillside where steep grassy slopes reach the top. Retrace your steps back to the main loop path, which makes for a pleasant but simple return to Tarbet.

Viking Raids

Between Loch Lomond and Loch Long (and the villages of Tarbet and Arrochar) is a narrow neck of land measuring approximately 2 miles. Famously, in 1263, the Vikings, led by the wonderfully named Haakon King of Man, carried their longships over this ground, having sailed up Loch Long from the sea, to reach Loch Lomond where they conducted a series of devastating raids. The ancient practice of dragging boats and their contents between bodies of water gave rise to the name Tarbet, which means 'the place of portage' and there are several similarly named settlements and lochs across Scotland.

Tarbet sunrise

Heath orchid

The Walk

Tarbet sits idyllically along the shores of Loch Lomond from where you are treated to a superb view of Ben Lomond's conical summit while the top of Cruach Tairbeirt rises above Tarbet's woodland to the north.

1. From the car park (where there is a café) cross the **A82**, turn left past the **Tarbet Hotel** then go right along the **A83** towards Arrochar. Follow this west for ½ a mile, passing a tearoom and a restaurant, to reach **Station Road**.

2. Turn right, signposted for Arrochar and Inveruglas, and follow the narrow road as it climbs to 'Arrochar and Tarbet Railway Station'. Walk through an **underpass** beneath the railway line.

From here a path climbs sharply into pleasant mixed woodland to gain a junction. Go right onto the **Cruach Tairbeirt Loop path** (which is waymarked with red marker posts throughout) and continue to climb steeply, soon passing a path on the right, which is the return route.

Once across a burn the incline eases and it is a lovely, easy walk northeast through the forest. In due course the path passes a bench, a good spot for a break, where a striking view of Ben Lomond can be enjoyed.

Having followed the forest path for just under a mile, a **firebreak** is reached on the left, waymarked with posts on either side.

Deep woods: *The Cruach Tairbeirt Loop is home to some beautiful woodland*

Here, an initially clear path rises gradually through the trees but it quickly becomes muddy and vague at points — boots will undoubtedly get wet here.

This boggy section is reasonably short-lived and in time the path improves, soon reaching a **burn** (a good point to clean your boots). This is easily crossed from where a much firmer path continues a steady ascent in a northwesterly direction, ascending out of the woodland onto open hillside at the 260-metre contour line. Above rise the steeper eastern slopes of **Cruach Tairbeirt**.

Almost immediately the path peters out so keep on towards a small pocket of conifers before heading west up steeper heathery slopes onto a flatter plateau, a little southeast below the main summit.

The ground here is home to heath orchid, harebell and clover. It is worth taking a breather to enjoy the view south along the island dotted waters of Loch Lomond.

From here a short climb up a rough, grassy path gains **Cruach Tairbeirt's**

Mountain high: *Panorama taking in Loch Long, The Brack and the incomparable Ben Arthur, better known as 'The Cobbler'*

spacious summit from where the path culminates at its trig point.

Here an extraordinary panorama opens out, particularly to the north and west — the Munro's of Beinn Narnain, Ben Vane, and Ben Vorlich (with Loch Sloy nestled inbetween the latter two) and the Corbett of The Brack rise sharply from Arrochar and the long finger of Loch Long. Loch Lomond is also visible with Ben Lomond standing guard, while the big jumble of muscular mountains above Crianlarich form an

impressive barrier. However it is the view of The Cobbler that is a real standout with its iconic profile and triumvirate of peaks clearly visible.

4. Retrace steps from the summit back down to the waymarked Cruach Tairbeirt Loop path at the edge of the firebreak (Point 3) and turn left. Follow this as it continues easily along a really lovely section of the route, dropping down to cross a **bridge over a burn.**

5. From here another attractive section descends above a **wooded ravine,** shortly swinging right to cross another **bridge.** The path now meanders its way

...through the forest, with a good view ...outh of Ben Reoch's steep incline.

...he path eventually swings sharp right ...nd makes a final climb to cross a **burn** ...here it joins the outward-bound route.

6. Turn left and retrace steps out of the forest to the **railway station** and back to **Tarbet**, to complete the walk. ♦

'Loch of the ships'

Loch Long's name has nothing to do with its length (although it does stretch for around 20 miles) but instead means 'Loch of ships'; this may relate to the boats that once navigated their way inland from the sea. Loch Long is one of a number of sea lochs that bite deep into Scotland's coastline and it was used as a secret torpedo testing ground during World War II.

Loch Lomond and its islands from the slopes of Beinn Dubh

Beinn Dubh & Mid Hill

The Luss Hills provide a wilder and remoter experience to hillwalking above Loch Lomond

What to expect:
Good paths along most of route. Section of pathless ground. Steep ascent/descent

Distance/time: 8.75 kilometres/7¼ miles. Allow 4¾ hours

Ascent/Descent: 738 metres/2,421 feet

Start: The large pay and display car park in Luss, which can get very busy, particularly during the summer months. Alternative parking is limited within the village

Grid ref: NS 359 931

Ordnance Survey Map: Explorer OL 38 Loch Lomond South Dumbarton & Helensburgh Drymen & Cove

After the walk: Pub and hotel in Luss

Walk outline

Beinn Dubh and Mid Hill, two of the Luss Hills that rise above Loch Lomond's western shore, combine to make a fabulous route. A good path climbs steeply from Luss village onto Beinn Dubh before rougher ground rises above Coire na h-Eanachan and the highest point of the route. Once across Mid Hill a steep path drops down into Glen Luss. A quiet scenic road leads back to Luss.

The Luss Hills

Sitting near the craggy Arrochar Alps and overlooked by the ever-popular Munro of Ben Lomond, the Luss Hills are vastly underrated and grant superb walking with wonderful far-reaching views. Bounded by Glen Fruin to the south and Glen Douglas to the north this lovely range of hills reach their high point of 713-metres at Beinn Chaorach. Glen Luss strikes through the heart of the Luss Hills. When up high the ruggedness of the upland topography, scored with deep V-shaped passes, wouldn't look out of place in the Lake District. The name Luss, from the Gaelic 'lus', means herb.

Glen Luss

Blaeberry, or bilberry

The Walk

1. From the **car park** walk to its southwestern corner then turn left at the **post office** onto the main **Luss Road**. Take the next road on the right, signposted for Glen Luss, then, after only a few metres, bear left, opposite **Luss Primary School**, and climb steps onto a **bridge** that crosses the A82.

2. At its end follow a narrow road past a house then bear right through a gate onto a path. Immediately turn right, cross a stile from where another path rises north across a field then through a pocket of **oak woodland**.

Beyond a gate the path climbs steeply across open hillside, eventually reaching the 250-metre contour line.

Here the gradient eases for a short spell, a good point to take a breather and revel in a fabulous view across Glen Luss to Coille-eughainn Hill, Beinn Chaorach and Beinn Eich.

3. A section of flatter boggy ground proceeds northwest but it improves underfoot once it begins to climb again.

A steep ascent now heads up the prominent southeastern shoulder of **Beinn Dubh**, with heather, tormentil and blaeberry (or bilberry) on the ground. Eventually the path picks up a line of fenceposts just below **Creag a t-Seilich**.

bove Loch Lomond: *The view from Beinn ubh extends over the National Park*

ook back for a wonderful view across och Lomond (its many islands mapped ut below) to Dumbarton Rock and the ver Clyde. On a clear day, Tinto Hill, some 0 miles to the southeast, is also visible.

ith the fence to the left the path gives n amazing view down into Glen Luss nd the farms of Glenmollochan and entaggart.

oon a stile takes you across the fence nd a gradual climb, with the fence

now on the right, leads towards the top. A couple of false summits make it frustrating for tired legs but the 642-metres summit cairn is soon gained.

Just beyond the cairn the full panorama is complete with a breathtaking view of the Arrochar Alps (Beinn Narnain and the Cobbler in particular), big Munro's such as Beinn Chabhair and An Caisteal above Crianlarich and a great outlook north along Loch Lomond to Ben Lomond.

4. With much of the hard work now done the scenery can really be enjoyed although it is only an intermittent path

Sunlight and shadow: *The Arrochar Alps and the mountains above Crianlarich dominate the view from Beinn Dubh*

that continues northwest across a flatter, boggier plateau.

Initially the fence posts provide a handrail but these soon peel away right. Now the terrain is a little rougher and featureless with the topography potentially problematic in poor visibility.

The path becomes more evident as a short climb west gains a **cairn above Coire na h-Eanachan**, at 657-metres the highest point of the route. Again the Arrochar Alps dominate while steep slopes drop north down into the narrow defile of Glen Douglas.

5. Continue easily southwest then southeast over the bump of **Mid Hill** after which a steeper drop, along a good path, descends **Mid Hill's southeastern ridge** above Glen Striddle — marvellous views extend along Glen Luss to Loch Lomond.

Once over a stile at a fence gradual slopes soon pass through a gate in a wall with a rough track then descending into **Glen Luss**. Once through a final gate turn left onto the narrow **Glen Luss Road**, just north of **Glenmollochan Farm**.

. Continue to a junction, keep left from where the road continues, with sporadic views of Loch Lomond. Keep an eye out or traffic as the road heads southeast, igh above Glen Luss and underneath he steep slopes of Beinn Dubh

7. After 2.75 kilometres, just before a cattle grid near **Luss**, bear left onto a path and follow this back to the gate at the base of Beinn Dubh. Once through retrace steps across the **A82 bridge** into Luss, to complete the walk. ♦

Bloody rivalry

Clan Colquhoun has held lands in and around Luss since the 1300s and during the 16th century the family lived in Rossdhu Castle (now a ruin) on the banks of Loch Lomond. The most infamous episode in the clan's history happened in 1603 when they met neighbouring Clan MacGregor in Glen Fruin where a bloody battle left the Colquhouns with 140 of their clan dead.

From Duncryne, the Southern Highlands and Ben Lomond rise above Loch Lomond

Duncryne

Small but perfectly formed, Duncryne grants an astonishing panorama of countryside, loch and mountain

Distance/time: 3.25 kilometres/2 miles. Allow 1 hour

Ascent/Descent: 102 metres/335 feet

Start: Kilmaronock Millennium Hall Car Park. Parking is free. Alternative parking is limited within the village

Grid ref: NS 429 862

Ordnance Survey Map: Explorer OL 38 Loch Lomond South Dumbarton & Helensburgh Drymen & Cove

After the walk: Coffee shop in Gartocharn, pubs/hotels in Drymen and Balloch

Walk outline

From the quiet confines of Gartocharn a narrow road leaves the village and soon reaches a little pocket of woodland, which itself leads to the base of Duncryne. From here it is a short but steep pull, along a good path, to gain the flat top of Duncryne and a view that far exceeds the little effort required to get there. The return is by the outward-bound route.

Duncryne

The late, great hillwalker and broadcaster Tom Weir lived much of his life in Gartocharn and climbed Duncryne almost every day (and sometimes at night). He described the summit view as the best from any small hill in Scotland and it is hard to disagree. Known locally (and perhaps a little disparagingly) as 'The Dumpling', due to its profile, Duncryne means 'the rounded hill-fort', and when on the summit it is easy to understand why it was once used as a defensive site. However the real history of Duncryne hill dates back some 350-million years — when it was formed through volcanic activity.

Evening light

Roe deer at dawn

The Walk

1. The route starts from the **Kilmaronock Car Park** in **Gartocharn** village centre, where there is a fine view of Duncryne's wooded profile.

Gartocharn means 'place of the humped hill', while Kilmaronock translates as 'the cell of little ronan'. Saint Ronan was a bishop of Bute who established a small church near Gartocharn during the 8th century.

Exit left onto **Church Road**, keeping to the pavement as it swings left to reach the **A811**.

2. Make a left then turn right onto **Duncryne Road** and follow the pavement southeast past some lovely single storey cottages.

When the pavement ends stick to the roadside verge (watch for traffic) as it climbs gently with Duncryne coming back into view. The road is flanked by farmland and it is a lovely, peaceful landscape to pass through.

Once past the entrance road for **East Cambusmoon** go through a gate on the left into **Duncryne Woodland** where roe deer may be seen.

3. Keep to the firm path that climbs gradually through this attractive pocket of mixed woodland. Beyond two gates a fenced path crosses a field to another gate at the base of **Duncryne**.

4. Once through, the path splits so keep right and begin the steady climb northeast up the hillside, which is scattered with oak and rowan and fine views open out towards the Campsie Fells. When the path sweeps left it rises north more steeply alongside gorse and fern to another fork. Take the left path from where a short final pull gains **Duncryne's summit** trig and an incredible panorama.

Below Gartocharn nestles comfortably amongst its rural confines, where fields spread north to reach Loch Lomond, it full width and many o its islands on display.

Loch view: Duncryne's summit panorama was a favourite of the broadcaster Tom Weir

...urrounding the loch is the great beacon of ...en Lomond, the distinctive ridge of Conic ...ill and the rounded Luss Hills, scored with ...eep glens. Beyond, the Cobbler's iconic ...rofile and the brawny Arrochar Alps draw ...e eye to a great procession of Southern ...ighland mountains. To the east the lowland landscape is broken by the long line of the Campsie Fells.

5. Having revelled in the magnificent scenery retrace steps, taking care on the initial steep descent, enjoying a final view of the Campsies before walking back to **Gartocharn**, to complete the walk. ♦

Right to roam?

Unusually for Scottish hills where the right to roam responsibly is recognised by the Land Reform Act (Scotland) 2003, Duncryne is private. However, access is allowed through an agreement between the landowner and the Scottish Executive for Environmental and Rural Affairs Department. The land is managed to conserve the character of this environmentally sensitive area. So please enjoy this fabulous route with care and consideration.

Seen from Conic Hill, Loch Lomond's islands trace the line of the Highland Boundary Fa

Conic Hill

Rising above Loch Lomond, Conic Hill offers one of the National Park's finest vantage points

What to expect:

Good paths with several steep ascents/descents. Path indistinct across Conic Hill

Distance/time: 7.25 kilometres/4½ miles. Allow 3 hours

Ascent/Descent: 400 metres/1,310 feet

Start: Large car park in the centre of Balmaha. Parking is free but can get very busy, particularly in summer. Alternative parking is limited within the village

Grid ref: NS 421 909

Ordnance Survey Map: Explorer OL 38 Loch Lomond South Dumbarton & Helensburgh Drymen & Cove

After the walk: Pub/hotel in Balmaha

Walk outline

A fine section of the West Highland Way leaves the village of Balmaha before climbing steeply to the base of Conic Hill's summit ridge. A path, which can be sketchy at times, leads up onto and over the 361-metre top where there is an astonishing panorama. The descent is wonderful, dropping over the marvellous Druim nam Buraich, back to Loch Lomond from where the West Highland Way returns to Balmaha.

The Highland Boundary Fault Line

Conic Hill straddles the Highland Boundary Fault line, a major fault zone that runs from Arran in the west to Stonehaven near Aberdeen. It separates the Highlands and Lowlands of Scotland and when you stand on Conic Hill the divide is instantly evident.

To the south flatter plains, broken only by the rolling line of the Campsie Fells, extend towards Glasgow and beyond while north the big, brawny mountains of the Southern Highlands vie for your attention: Ben Lomond, the Arrochar Alps (especially the iconic profile of the 'Cobbler') and the Crianlarich Hills form a mighty and impressive barrier.

Conic Hill

Raven

The Walk

1. From the large **car park at Balmaha** (where Conic Hill's lumpy ridge rises sharply above) walk to its northeastern end where there is a large 'Balmaha' sign and **information board**.

Beyond both turn right onto the **West Highland Way** and follow a good solid path that makes its way, for 300 metres, through attractive mixed woodland of the **Queen Elizabeth Forest Park** to a track on the left. This climbs steadily for another 400 metres where a gate leads out of the forest into open countryside.

2. Keep along the West Highland Way, which soon begins to climb sharply northwest, leading up and through **Bealach Ard** (Pass of the Height). The path is flanked with hawthorn and rowan, where steps make the going a little easier. It leads to a viewpoint and a marvellous vista towards the Campsie Fells.

The path now ascends steadily through Bealach Ard (where lovely scatterings of bog cotton are prevalent), in due course climbing over a crest to reach a West Highland Way marker post.

Keep on along the superbly maintained path, ascending towards the knobbly **summit ridge of Conic Hill**. *You will see (and hear) ravens swooping above and fantastic views across Loch Lomond open out.*

Once past the westernmost domed **top of Conic Hill** leave the West Highland Way by taking a prominent path on the right.

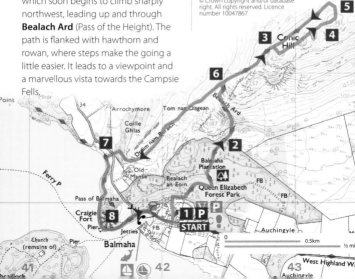

rchetypal scene?: *Long horned Highland*
ttle above Druim nam Buraich

This ascends steeply to reach a dip
between two of Conic Hill's heather
ad knolls. Go right and walk the short
stance to its westernmost top.

om here a stunning view along Loch
omond (with the islands of Inchailloch
nd Inchmurrin sitting on the Highland
oundary Fault Line) opens out, extending
Gare Loch and the extraordinary, jagged
rofile of Arran.

etrace steps past the outward-bound

path and continue northeast along the
summit ridge. The path becomes a little
faint at times as progress is made but
the **highest point of Conic Hill** is soon
reached, its 361-metre summit marked
with a **small cairn**.

Again the view is expansive and
spectacular, with Ben Lomond and The
Cobbler particularly prominent, as is the
distinct contrast of landscape to the south
and north of the Highland Boundary.

4. Keep on a northeast bearing,
following a faint animal path that drop
steadily back to the West Highland Way.

Hills and islands: *Loch Lomond's islands draw the eye to Arran's jagged outline*

5. Turn left and follow this underneath Conic Hill, all the way back to the West Highland Way post above Bealach Ard.

6. Here the path splits; take the right fork, leaving the West Highland Way, and follow a grassy path along a wonderful **ridge** above a lovely little glen. This undulating ridge descends southwest with the path soon swinging right onto **Druim nam Buraich**, another eye-catching ridge that offers a dazzling view of Inchcailloch and of Conic Hill.

In due course the path begins to drop steeply, zigzagging down into tranquil woodland where the incline eases. Continue through the wood to a gate beside the **Balmaha/Rowardennan road**.

7. Once through, cross the road, go through another gate, cross a field and after another gate turn left back onto the West Highland Way.

Follow this along a scenic section of **Loch Lomond** for 500 metres at which point the West Highland Way turns left.

8. Leave it behind by going straight on, following a path along the

chside, which in turn crosses a metal **otbridge**, taking you over the loch side a steep cliff face. A short, rockier ction of path culminates at a **jetty** th **Inchcailloch** nearby out on the ch.

Turn left onto a quiet minor road (keep an eye out for traffic) that leads back into **Balmaha**. At the **B837** bear right and follow a lochside path then pavement back to the start, to complete the walk.◆

Woods and water

The Queen Elizabeth Forest Park extends across much of Loch Lomond and The Trossachs National Park, cloaking the slopes of Ben Lomond, Ben Ledi and Ben A'an. It is pierced by great bodies of water such as Loch Katrine and Loch Ard. Wildlife at home in the forest includes red and roe deer, red squirrels, pine martens and sparrowhawks. Out on the moors, watch for curlews, lapwings, golden plovers and short-eared owls.

Looking down on the David Marshall Lodge from Craigmore

Craigmore

*he Trossach's magnificent scenery is particularly breath-
aking during this ascent to the summit of Craigmore*

What to expect:
*Waymarked woodland
paths, steep path onto
Craigmore. Indistinct,
rough path on descent*

istance/time: 6.5 kilometres/4 miles. Allow 2½ hours

scent/Descent: 380 metres/1,263 feet

art: Large car park in the centre of Aberfoyle beside The Tros-
chs Discovery Centre

rid ref: NN 522 009

rdnance Survey Map: Explorer OL 46 The Trossachs, *Callander,
erfoyle & Lochearnhead, Balquhidder & Strathyre*

ter the walk: Pubs/hotel in Aberfoyle

alk outline

n the outskirts of Aberfoyle, a waymarked trail leads through
arvellous oak woodland to arrive at an impressive waterfall.
om here a steady climb gains the Duke's Pass and the lower
opes of Craigmore. A decent path ascends steeply onto
aigmore's 387-metre summit and a splendid panorama. The
urn path is initially steep and rough but beyond the David
arshall Lodge a waymarked trail leads back to Aberfoyle..

erfoyle

day's rural idyll belies Aberfoyle's development during
industrial past. Slate quarrying and an oak charcoal
dustry were important in the expansion of the village
ring the 19th century; prior to this, Aberfoyle was simply
mall settlement straddling the banks of the River Forth.
n ore production was at its height during the 18th and
th centuries (Aberfoyle also had an iron market some
0 years ago) and its first quarry opened in 1858. When
e railway arrived in 1882 the village (which by then had
ur quarries) became the third largest supplier of slate in
otland.

Little Fawn Falls

Pine marten

The Walk

1. Walk west through the car park to **Manse Road**, turn right then right again onto **Lochard Road** (B829). Go next left onto the **Duke's Pass** (A821), which begins to climb sharply away from Aberfoyle.

Originally built in the 19th century by the Duke of Montrose to improve access to his estate, the Duke's Pass was subsequently utilised by Victorian tourists after Sir Walter Scott's epic poem 'The Lady of the Lake' put The Trossachs on the map.

2. After approximately 400 metres the pavement ends; bear right here, up steps into **woodland**.

Following green waymarks, take the firs path on the right, then go right again a a junction. Walk downhill for 250 metre turning left when the track splits.

After a short incline, turn right and follow a path that loops through an **oa coppiced enclosure**.

Once out of the enclosure, follow the **riverbank path** above the **Allt a' Mhangan**, eventually reaching a junction. Turn right and continue to a **wooden bridge** spanning the river.

3. Don't cross, instead turn left and, wit the river to the right, continue upstream in full view of the 16-metre high **Little Fawn Falls**. The path veers left and the shortly afterwards splits. Keep right her onto a blue waymarked path that wind steeply uphill.

Once across a **little stone bridge**, turn right and continue to ascend steadily up to the **Duke's Pass.**

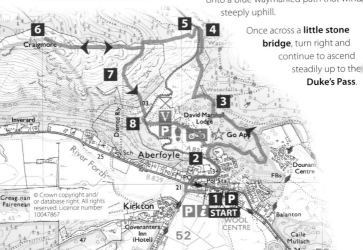

ol burn: The cascading waters of the Allt Mhangan

Go straight across onto another path, which zigzags up the lower slopes of **aigmore** with fine views opening out ross the Trossachs to Ben Ledi. Further , it reaches a path on the left with ue waymarked posts on either side.

Take this and climb steeply to reach slate embankment and the **old amway**, which was used to link the te quarries with Aberfoyle.

mb onto the embankment, turn left,

then after 20 metres go right onto a path that begins to rise steadily west towards the summit. It can be a little boggy but superb views extend over Aberfoyle to the Campsie Fells. After a short descent, the path makes its final climb onto the **broad summit**.

Only now is the true extent of Craigmore's outstanding panorama revealed: Ben Lomond, The Cobbler, Ben More, Stob Binnien, Ben Venue and Loch Ard are prominent, while on a clear day the view extends along Flanders Moss to Stirling, its castle and the Wallace Monument.

Forests and water: *Ben Lomond dominates the view from the summit of Craigmore*

6. Return to the tramway, turn right and traverse **Craigmore**, high above Aberfoyle.

7. After 250 metres the tramway ends abruptly and a narrow path begins to drop steeply southeast.

During summer it can be overgrown, covering rougher ground underfoot so care should be taken. In time the path drops into woodland, crosses a low fence then concludes at the **A821** near **David Marshall Lodge**.

8. Go right then left onto the David Marshall Lodge access road (the lodge has a **café**, **shop** and **information centre**). When it splits keep right and just before the visitor centre turn right onto a waymarked path. Follow this pa[th] a **statue** commemorating the Women's Timber Corp (1942-46).

Affectionately known as Lumberjills, the Woman's Timber Corp worked throughou[t] the country during World War II, carrying out arduous tasks, such as felling and sawmilling timber, that had historically been the domain of men. The statue recognises their dedication that was crucial to the war effort.

The path drops gently downhill for

...ome time to a T-junction. Go right here ...hen at the next junction, right again, ...ear Little Fawn Falls. Here a paved path ...ontinues to a path on the left, which in ...urn regains the outward-bound route

on the outskirts of Aberfoyle. Once out of the woodland, turn left and return to **Aberfoyle**, to complete the walk. ♦

Hearts of oak

Aberfoyle's oak woodland was coppiced every 15-20 years during the four centuries that the land was owned by the Duke of Montrose. Coppicing encourages new growth and, consequently, a regularly coppiced tree will never die of old age. Oak trees in Britain are home to more insects than any other tree. Walking here, look out for woodland birds, including chaffinches, treecreepers, jays and wood warblers.

The impressive Little Fawn Falls

Lime Craig

Rising above Aberfoyle, Lime Craig provides stunning scenery and interesting history in equal measure

What to expect:
Waymarked trail through forest, one steep descent. Steep climb onto Lime Craig

Distance/time: 6.75 kilometres/4¼ miles. Allow 2½ hours

Ascent/Descent: 336 metres/1,102 feet

Start: Large car park in the centre of Aberfoyle beside The Trossachs Discovery Centre

Grid ref: NN 522 009

Ordnance Survey Map: Explorer OL 46 The Trossachs, *Callander, Aberfoyle & Lochearnhead, Balquhidder & Strathyre*

After the walk: Pubs/hotel in Aberfoyle

Walk outline

Beginning from Aberfoyle, the pavement rises from the village to reach the Queen Elizabeth Forest Park. Here the waymarked Lime Craig Trail (also known as the Highland Boundary Fault Trail) rises to the base of Lime Craig. It is then a steep path to gain the summit and its wonderful panorama. The return journey utilises the steep wagon way, which provides clues to the industry that contributed to Aberfoyle's development.

Lime Quarrying

Lime Craig stands at the western edge of the Menteith Hills, which form a prominent marker above Aberfoyle. The lime quarry can still be seen beneath the summit of Lime Craig, with the rock composite containing the likes of Dalradian Slate and Lower Old Red Sandstone.

During the early 19th century the quarried limestone was transported along an inclined railway line, where wooden wagons carried their load to lime kilns at the base of the hill.

National Cycle Network sign

Part of this walk follows the course of the line. By 1850 the quarry had run its course and work came to an end.

Red squirrel

The Walk

1. Walk west through the car park to **Manse Road**, turn right then right again onto **Lochard Road** (B829). Go next left onto the **Duke's Pass** (A821), which begins to climb sharply away from **Aberfoyle**.

2. After approximately 400-metres the pavement ends and here bear right up **steps into woodland**.

Initially following green waymarks, keep on the path as it sweeps left (ignoring a path on the right) to a junction. Go right where a **paved path** (part of the National Cycle Network (**NCN 7**) heads north through the woodland onto the red waymarked **Lime Craig Trail**.

It soon passes a distinctive blue NCN marker post to reach a **wooden footbridge** spanning the **Allt a' Mhangan**.

A little to the left is the impressive **Little Fawn Falls**, which drop 16 metres through an impressive gorge. A visit is well worth the short detour.

3. Once across the **bridge** turn left at a junction onto a **wide forestry track** and continue on a steady ascent for 350-metres to another junction. Go

ream stream: *The Allt a' Mhangan travels through lovely oak woodland*

eft again from where the firm track maintains its ascent.

runs through predominantly larch and pruce woodland where dunnock, coal tit nd willow warbler may be spied.

n due course the gradient lessens as the rack passes **another lovely waterfall** – there is a **bench** here making it a ood spot for a break. Keep on as the oute curves right to reach a crossroads.

. Make a right here from where an easy

level section runs beneath an impressive forest canopy, particularly attractive during autumn.

As it sweeps left the track crosses the Highland Boundary Fault Line and a final push along a steady ascent, before long reaching the **base of Lime Craig**, beside a junction of paths. The sheer slope of the quarried face climbs sharply ahead.

5. Take the well-worn path on the left (leaving the trail behind), which rises steeply. *The slopes of Lime Craig are scattered with rowan and birch.*

Soon after the path swings right, the

Sun and space: *From Lime Craig the rugged slopes of Ben Vane and Ben Ledi rise above the Queen Elizabeth Forest Park*

incline eases a little and passes a gate on the left (this takes you onto rougher ground of the Menteith Hills with the rounded heather-clad slopes of Craig of Monievreckie high above). Shortly afterwards the path splits, so keep right and make the final, simple climb onto **Lime Craig's 310-metre top**.

The view from the summit highlights the distinct natural features on either side of the Highland Boundary Fault. To the south the flatter plains of Flanders Moss draw the eye to the Campsie Fells and the Fintry Hills while to the north the Highlands rise sharply: Ben Vane and Ben Ledi climb above little Loch Drunkie, Ben Venue, Craigmore and Ben Lomond are all impressive while the quartet of big Munros above Crianlarich — Ben More, Stob Binnein, Cruach Ardrain and Beinn Tulaichean — strike skywards.

6. Retrace your steps back to the main trail at the base of Lime Craig. Go left, again following the red waymarks, onto the **old wagon way,** which drops sharply southwest through woodland — *watch out for red squirrels here, as well as admiring the fine view of Craigmore's domed summit through the trees.*

...art way down, the path crosses a ...ack, then continues dropping steeply ...owards Aberfoyle, to another track.

... Here turn right and follow this ...hrough more attractive forestry for 850 metres, all the way back to the **wooden footbridge** crossing the **Allt a' Mhangan**.

Once across, retrace your steps back into **Aberfoyle** to complete the walk. ♦

Rock band?

The Lime Craig Trail crosses the Highland Boundary Fault, a geological divide that separates the Scottish Highlands from the Lowlands. The raised fault runs from Arran, in the southwest, to Stonehaven near Aberdeen, in the northeast. It formed around 390 million years ago when what is known as the Shatter Zone pushed the older rocks of the Highlands upwards while the more youthful Lowland topography was pressed down.

The shapely profile of Ben Ledi from Ben Gullipen

Ben Gullipen

A straightforward ascent to the top of Ben Gullipen reveals magnificent loch and mountain views

What to expect:
Wide track all the way to the summit along a steady climb

Distance/time: 4.75 kilometres/3 miles. Allow 1½ hours

Ascent/Descent: 228 metres/748 feet

Start: Lay-by on the east side of the A81, 3.2 miles southwest of Callander and 8.1 miles northeast of Aberfoyle

Grid ref: NS 617 047

Ordnance Survey Map: Explorer OL 46 The Trossachs, *Callander, Aberfoyle & Lochearnhead, Balquhidder & Strathyre*

After the walk: Pubs/hotel in Aberfoyle and Callander

Walk outline

A wide track climbs steadily from the A81 through conifer woodland, eventually rising above the treeline and onto open hillside. The track continues its ascent all the way to the top of Ben Gullipen. The summit is marred by a radio mast but this is easily ignored by exploring the summit plateau and taking in the superb panorama. Return by the route of ascent.

Ben Gullipen

Scotland's mountain names often offer an interesting insight into the heritage and culture of our ancestors and Ben Gullipen is no different. A simple translation is thought to be 'great, rough hill'; but Peter Drummond, in his fascinating book *Scottish Hill and Mountain Names* asserts that Ben Gullipen may have its root in the name Gulbin – which suggests a close association to the Fingalian heroes. There are several similarly named hills in Scotland (including Beinn Ghuilbin near Aviemore) and it's said their slopes are the final resting places for the Fingalian warrior Diarmaid, his lover Grainne and their two hounds.

Through the forest

Bee on heather

The Walk

1. From the lay-by on the east side of the **A81** (where there is room for 5 or 6 cars), carefully cross the road, turn right then go through a metal gate on the left. Here a wide track climbs steadily northwest through **conifer woodland**.

As progress is made the angle of the ascent eases somewhat providing a pleasant walk through the trees.

During autumn there are several species of fungi, including the delicate porcelain fungi and the distinctive red-topped fly agaric, enjoying the shadier, damper confines of the forest.

Keep on the main track as it passes another track on the right and after 1.2 kilometres the tree cover is left behind.

2. Beyond a gate the route continues southwest across open hillside. *After the confines of the forest the views of the Southern Highlands are striking, while the*

town of Callander can be seen a little to the northeast. The summit of Ben Gullipen can also be seen ahead.

In due course, the track swings right and drops down across a **burn** from where it begins to rise steeply. After veering to the left a final approach of 600 metres climbs gradually to gain the 414-metre **summit**.

At its western end, beyond the large **radio mast**, a stile crosses a fence from where the plateau can be easily explored.

The view is fantastic. Lochan Balloch sits below the summit while the long finger of Loch Venachar draws the eye to the Menteith Hills, Ben Venue, Ben A'an and much of The Trossachs. Way to the east the rolling line of the Ochil Hills stand guard over the Wallace Monument and Stirling Castle. To the northwest the pointed

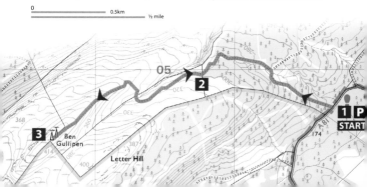

stant view: *The town of Callander is* *arly visible from the slopes of Ben Gullipen*

ak of Ben More and the flat-topped *ob Binnein are prominent as are the* *in Munros of Ben Vorlich and Stuc a* *roin a little to the east. However it is the* *'9-metre high Ben Ledi that really stands* *t. It rises sharply from the north shore* *Loch Venachar and from Ben Gullipen's*

lower vantage point you get a real sense of its size, shape and bulk. It is an impressive mountain, and one of Scotland's 222 Corbetts (Scottish mountains between 2500-2999 feet).

3. It is now a simple matter of retracing your steps back to the start, enjoying the marvellous views across Stirlingshire, to complete the walk. ♦

Summer skylarks

Like many of Scotland's hills and mountains Ben Gullipen is home to that ubiquitous upland bird, the skylark. This attractive but nervy little brown bird is instantly recognisable because of its rapid wing beats followed by a longer glide, as well as its loud trills when in flight or when alarmed. It is often confused with the smaller but equally charming moorland bird — the meadow pipit.

The view along Loch Katrine from Ben A'an is superb

Ben A'an

en A'an is a hill walking classic with a view that hugely utweighs any effort to reach the top

What to expect:
Well-worn path through woodland then steep climb onto Ben A'an's summit

Distance: 3.75 kilometres/2¼ miles. Allow 2¼ hours

scent/Descent: 340 metres/1,115 feet

art: Pay and display Forestry Commission Ben A'an Car Park, which sits 2 miles west from the village of Brig o'Turk

rid ref: NN 509 070

rdnance Survey Map: Explorer Explorer OL46 Callander, *Aberfoyle Lochearnhead, Balquhidder & Strathyre*

fter the walk: Pub in Brig o'Turk, hotel at Loch Achray

alk outline

though this route is steep, it is short and an ideal troduction for younger children to hillwalking. Beginning om the Ben A'an Car Park, at the head of Loch Achray, the alk rises through gorgeous woodland to the base of Ben an's prominent cone. A steep ascent up a clear, at times oggy, path soon reaches the summit. The return journey is by e route of ascent.

en A'an

here is an old adage that the best views are from the wer vantage points and this is certainly true of Ben A'an, wonderful, diminutive peak that rises to 461 metres bove the Loch Lomond and The Trossachs National Park. is rocky pinnacle has real mountain character, and its rtiginous higher flanks have been popular with climbers r decades; particularly during the 1930s, when the great orking class outdoor movement began. Workers would tch hike to the hills surrounding Loch Lomond where ey would spend their entire weekend climbing before turning to work on the Monday.

Ben A'an summit

Golden eagle

The Walk

1. From the car park carefully cross the **A821**, after which take a wide track that ascends north over steep ground.

Recently many of the non-native species of trees that once clung to the lower slopes of Ben A'an have been cleared, to make way for indigenous varieties and to improve the ascent. Subsequently fine views across Loch Achray have opened out.

Loch Achray translates, somewhat mysteriously, as 'the loch of the ford of

shaking'. The shaking may relate to the boggy ground that once stood between Loch Achray and Loch Katrine while the ford would have been near the mouth of the Achray Water as it enters Loch Achray.

As the climb continues a path heads northwest alongside the cascading waters of the **Allt Inneil**.

2. Once the burn is crossed via a **wooden footbridge**, keep climbing along the burn's northern bank.

Keep an eye out for dippers flitting amongst the streamside rocks. Other wildlife to look out for includes roe and red deer, red squirrel, redstart and wood warbler, while the prints of the elusive pine marten may well be seen. Bluebell, primrose and wood anemone are scattere across the woodland floor.

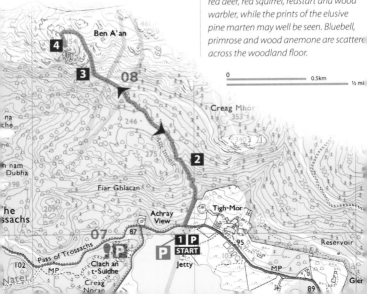

Climb every mountain: *Relaxing on the summit of Ben A'an*

keep on as the path continues its steady ascent, crossing the Allt Inneil for a second time.

Now the walk proceeds through beautiful birchwoods. Here the reward for your exertions is a superb view of Ben A'an's distinctive sharp upper reaches.

The path exits the woods at the 300-metre contour line with the seemingly impenetrable slopes of Ben

A'an rising precipitously above. However a rocky but clear path heads north above the treeline, affording a superb outlook towards Ben Venue and the glassy waters of Loch Katrine.

Although a little boggy at times, the steepness of the ascent causes no major problems for most walkers, and younger kids will revel in the mountainous nature of the walk.

On the higher, rocky ledges, near the summit of Ben A'an, are the bright purple flowers of wild thyme. These beautiful little pink flowers form conspicuous mats

Small packages?: *Ben A'an's mountain character matches many of the far bigger, bulkier hills of the Southern Highlands*

and are most visible between May and August. By rubbing the flower or leaves the distinctive scent of thyme is released.

The path picks its way through a rugged landscape and the steepness of the route eventually relents. The final stage of the climb rises gradually across heathery hillside, heading west then south onto the craggy 461-metre high summit.

The view from the top of this pocket-sized peak is truly astonishing. Below, the waters

of Loch Achray and Loch Venachar are framed by the likes of Ben Venue, Ben Ledi and the Menteith Hills while on a clear day the Wallace Monument above Stirling may be visible. Heading west and the long arm of Loch Katrine draws the eye to the Arrochar Alps and beyond, to the big, brutish hills of the Southern and Central Highlands.

This view has been admired ever since the tourist boom of the early 19th century and would have been relished by climbing pioneers, such as Jock Nimlin, who utilised Ben A'an's vertiginous slopes to practice their climbing skills, before hitting the bigger mountains of the West Highlands

…uring the great working class outdoor …novement of the 1930s. Ben A'an is still a …opular haunt for climbers today.

…. The only feasible means of return is …o come back by the route of ascent,

taking care on the steep descent down into the birch woodland. However, with superb views across the Trossachs and the wildlife-rich woodland, it is a joy throughout. ♦

Poetic licence?

It was Sir Walter Scott who, mistakenly, named Ben A'an when writing his epic poem, The Lady of the Lake. *He actually spelled it Ben-an and it seems he may have copied the bracketed version of Am Binnean as it appeared on the Ordnance Survey map of the day. It is thought that Am Binnean translates, appropriately, as 'the small pointed peak'.*

The Jubilee Cairn at the top of Callander Craig

Callander Craig

Callander Craig rises above Callander and, when combined with Bracklinn Falls, grants a marvellously scenic walk

What to expect:
Pavement, minor road, firm but steep hillside path. Rough path across summit

Distance/time: 8 kilometres/5 miles. Allow 2½ hours

Ascent/Descent: 289 metres/948 feet

Start: Callander Meadows Car Park (free), on western edge of town. OR Callander Crag or Bracklinn Falls car parks (both free), respectively 0.5km and 0.75km north of Main Street on Bracklinn Road.

Grid ref: NN 630 078

Ordnance Survey Map: Explorer OL 46 The Trossachs, *Callander, Aberfoyle & Lochearnhead, Balquhidder & Strathyre*

After the walk: Pubs/hotel in Callander

Walk outline

This delightful walk leaves the bustling town of Callander for the fine network of forest tracks and hillside paths that gain the long summit ridge of Callander Craig. This high ground bestows magnificent views across Stirlingshire, the highlands of central Scotland and Loch Lomond and The Trossachs National Park. A quiet, picturesque road leads back towards Callander and allows for a short detour to see the spectacular Bracklinn Falls.

Callander

The lively and bustling town of Callander stands at the edge of the Highlands and is the eastern gateway to the Loch Lomond and The Trossachs National Park. It has been an important settlement ever since the Romans established a fort here at the edge of the River Teith, naming it *Bochastle*. It continued to develop, particularly when Major Caulfeild's military road passed through Callander in the 18th century. It then became a major tourist destination with the arrival of the railway in 1858, and it remains so today.

Callander Craig woodland

Ringlet butterfly

A force of nature: *The spectacular Bracklinn Falls near Callendar*

The Walk

Callander Meadows Car Park stands on the banks of the River Teith, making for a scenic start to this walk with the mountain of Ben Ledi looking particularly striking from this angle. The river is considered to be one of the finest for salmon and trout fishing in Scotland.

1. From the car park turn right onto **Callander Main Street** (A84) and walk through the **town** for just under 0.75km to reach **Bracklin Road** (signposted for Callander Crags and Bracklinn Falls).

Turn left from where the narrow road climbs steadily to a junction. Keep left and continue to **Callander Crags car park**.

2. Walk through the car park then go round a barrier onto a wide **forestry track**, which rises gradually, following red waymarks. Look out for red squirrels as you climb for 150 metres to a waymarked path on the right.

Follow this as it winds steeply uphill. In

while it sweeps left, passing a path on
the right, from where the steep ascent
passes a **picnic table**.

*This is a good spot for a breather as there
are fine views across Callander to the
Campsie Fells and Ben Gullipen.*

Once through a small pocket of
attractive beech trees the base of the
impressive crags is reached. Beyond
a **bench** the path climbs much more
steeply although rough stone steps
help make the ascent a little easier.
This culminates on the main ridge of
Callander Craig beside a **bridge**.

3. Turn right across this and walk
northeast along the top of the crag,
which is scattered with lovely stands
of birch, rowan and Scots Pine.
The path runs right of a fence
and there are a couple

of slabby sections of rock to cross —
although not problematic, hands and
feet may be required.

The gradual ascent passes through a
gate and soon reaches the 343-metre
summit of Callander Craig, which is
adorned by the tall **Queen Victoria
Jubilee Cairn**. *This was erected in 1897 by
Malcolm Ferguson of Callander.*

*All along the ridge the views are superb.
To the north a high, rugged mattress
of wild moorland draws the eye to the
shapely Munros of Stuc a Chroin and Ben
Vorlich while west the great bulk of Ben
Ledi fills the view. The long narrow line of*

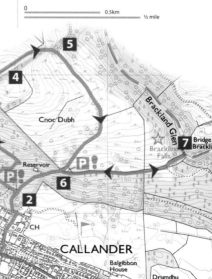

Brown study?: *Callander Crag's summit view draws the eye to the Munros Stuc a Chroin and Ben Vorlich*

Loch Venachar sits below. To the south the slopes of the crag drop steeply down to a gorgeous rural landscape that extends all the way to the Ochils, Stirling Castle, the Wallace Monument and the Forth Estuary.

4. From the **cairn** continue northeast across the summit and soon the path begins to descend. Again a couple of **rocky shelves** make it a little awkward but beyond this a straightforward, if a little muddy, descent continues with further superb views of Stuc a Chroin and Ben Vorlich.

In due course the path drops steeply through a lovely little pocket of **birch woodland** to reach a **narrow road** (an extension of Bracklin Road)

5. Turn right and follow this quiet road that provides easy, scenic walking with the view extending to the Campsie Fells and Stirling.

6. After 1 kilometre it drops down to gain **Bracklinn Falls Car Park** on the left. For an optional but worthwhile **detour** walk through the car park then turn left onto a path.

This is easily followed through more attractive woodland for 600 metres

...here it sweeps left then zigzags down to the **Keltie Water** and the fabulous **Bracklinn Falls**. This is an impressive (and after heavy rain) noisy spot as the waterfall plunges through the gorge.

7. Retrace steps back to the car park then turn left onto **Bracklin Road**. This is followed past **Callander Crags car park**. Retrace your steps back to **Callander**, to complete the walk. ♦

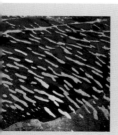

'Speckled pool'

The word bracklinn translates from Gaelic as 'the speckled pool', in this case relating to the deep plunge pool tucked in at the base of the Bracklinn Falls. The gorge was reshaped during flash floods in 2004, which raised the level of the water by 50 feet, sweeping away the old bridge spanning the Keltie Water. It was not until 2010 that the present day bridge opened.

The lower slopes of Beinn an t-Sithein give a fantastic view along Loch Lubnaig

Beinn an t-Sidhein

Beinn an t-Sidhein's summit grants a wilder and glorious viewpoint across the Southern Highlands

What to expect:
Minor road, steep forestry and hillside paths. Rough path across summit

Distance/time: 7.75 kilometres/4¾ miles. Allow 3 hours

Ascent/Descent: 522 metres/1,713 feet

Start: Forestry Commission Car Park, which sits at the southern edge of Strathyre. Parking is free

Grid ref: NN 560 169

Ordnance Survey Map: Explorer OL 46 The Trossachs, *Callander, Aberfoyle & Lochearnhead, Balquhidder & Strathyre*

After the walk: Pubs/café in Strathyre

Walk outline

Beinn an t-Sidhein (pronounced Ben Shee-han) rises above the attractive village of Strathyre. A good path climbs steeply through Strathyre Forest onto open hillside from where a boggier stretch of path reaches the top of An t-Sidhein. It then extends across rougher, heather clad moorland onto Beinn an t-Sidhein and an incredible panorama across a mountainous landscape. Forest tracks and minor road return to Strathyre.

Strathyre

It is thought that Strathyre means 'twisting valley' and certainly the River Balvag winds its way through Strathyre's tight confines. It was part of the main droving route between the Highlands and Lowlands during the 17th century while Strathyre village became a popular tourist destination with the arrival of the Callander to Oban railway in the 1870s. The poet Duguld Buchanan was born in Strathyre in 1716. He helped the Reverend James Stewart of Killin translate the *New Testament* into Scottish Gaelic and wrote an important collection of Gaelic religious poems. A monument to Buchanan stands in the village.

Buchanan monument

Sundew

The Walk

1. The **Forestry Commission car park** stands at the southern end of Strathyre just off the A84. At the back of the car park, turn left onto a cycle/walkway (signed 'Falls of Leny and Callander') and follow this alongside the **River Balvag** that runs between Loch Voil and Loch Lubnaig.

Cross a **suspension bridge** that spans the river then go right onto a blue waymarked path and follow this to a minor road. Turn right, walk past several cottages. Beyond **Strathyre Primary School** follow a path on the left that runs parallel with the road.

2. After 100 metres (just before a junction) go left onto a waymarked path which climbs steeply into **Strathyre Forest** — *keep an eye out for red squirrels*. Upon reaching a track turn right and follow this gently uphill for a further 100 metres then bear left onto another path.

3. Again this climbs very steeply but it isn't long before it leads above the treeline where wonderful views across Strathyre to Beinn Each and along **Loch Lubnaig** open out.

Loch Lubnaig is approximately 3½ miles long and is thought to translate from Gaelic as 'Loch of the Bend'. The Corbett of Ben Ledi rises steeply from its southern edge.

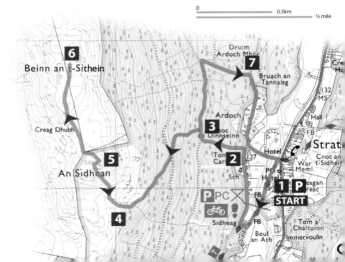

...dging the gap: *Crossing the suspension ...dge over the River Balvag*

...e stony path now takes a steadier ...cent and as height is gained the ...gged summit of Stuc a Chroin can be ...en to the east. Keep on uphill, soon ...ering right to run alongside a small **...nifer plantation**. A grassy, boggy ...th, which can be a little vague, now ...ntinues through scatterings of conifer.

...As a **low crag** is passed on the right, ...ep right onto a narrow path (marked ...th a **small pile of stones**) from where ...other steep rise begins. It climbs to

the left of the crag before continuing up grassy hillside, with the sharp slopes of An t-Sidhein above. Again the path can be vague but as it reaches a flatter, heathery plateau it becomes clearer. A final, zigzagging climb gains the **summit of An t-Sidhein**.

At 546-metres An t-Sidhein grants a breathtaking view. The rounded shape of Beinn an t-Sidhein rises a little to the north, with Strathyre and the River Balvag, hemmed in by steep hillside, drawing the eye to Loch Earn and the huge bulk of Ben Lawers. However it is the view east to Ben

Distant hills: *The mighty Crianlarich mountains from Beinn an t-Sidhein*

Vorlich and Stuc a Chroin and west to the long line of jagged Crianlarich Munros that really catches the eye.

5. Drop back down to the plateau, from where a rough path heads northwest over heather moorland to a stile in a fence. Once over, the path descends then rises across marshy ground onto the **twin-topped Beinn an t-Sidhein** — at 572-metres its northern top is the summit.

Again the view is absolutely stunning. The lonely landscape of Glen Buckie sits way

below Beinn an t-Sidhein while beyond Stob Binnein, Ben More, Cruach Ardrain and Beinn Tulaichean, above Crianlarich, take centre stage.

6. Retrace steps all the way back to the main forestry track in **Strathyre Forest** (Point 3), taking care on the steep sections of descent. Turn left and follow the track north for 400 metres to gain a junction.

Turn right onto another track and drop gradually downhill. After rounding a **barrier** go right onto a minor road.

7. This leads through more gorgeous **woodland**, on the outskirts of Strathyr

– there is also a good view up to the steep ~~s~~opes of An t-Sidhein.

~~U~~pon reaching a junction, just north of ~~S~~trathyre Primary School, turn left, follow ~~t~~he road back into the village, crossing a **stone bridge** over the **River Balvag** then turn right onto a **cycle/walkway** (signposted 'Village Centre'). Walk along here, back to the start, to complete the walk. ♦

Spirited country?

Folklore crops up in many mountain names, including Beinn an t-Sidhein, which means 'Fairy Mountain'. Robert Kirk, who was born in 1644 near Strathyre, in Aberfoyle, documented many of these stories during his life. However it wasn't until 1815 (over 120 years after his death) that Sir Walter Scott published Kirk's work in a book called The Secret Commonwealth. *It is still in print today.*

Useful Information

Loch Lomond and The Trossachs Tourism

Visit Scotland's official website covers everything from accommodation and events to attractions and adventure. **www.visitscotland.com/destinations-maps/loch-lomond-trossachs-forth-valley/**

Loch Lomond and The Trossachs National Park

The Loch Lomond and the Trossachs National Park website also has information on thing to see and do, plus maps, webcams and news. **www.lochlomond-trossachs.org/**

Tourist Information Centres

The main TICs provide free information on everything from accommodation and travel to what's on and walking advice.

Aberfoyle	01877 382 221	info@visitscotland.com
Balloch	01389 753 533	info@visitscotland.com
Balmaha	01389 722 100	info@lochlomond-trossachs.org
Callander	01877 330 342	info@visitscotland.com
Luss	01436 860 229	purdiesofluss@hotmail.co.uk

Emergencies

Loch Lomond and the Trossachs National Park is covered by the Lomond Mountain Rescue Team (**www.lomondmrt.org.uk**). In a real emergency:

1. Make a note of your location (with OS grid reference, if possible); the name, age and sex of the casualty; their injuries; how many people are in the group; and your mobile phone number.

2. Call 999 or 112 and ask for Police Scotland, and then for Mountain Rescue.

3. Give them your prepared details.

4. Do NOT change position until contacted by the mountain rescue team.

Weather

Three day weather forecast for Loch Lomond and The Trossachs National Park: **www.mwis.org.uk/scottish-forecast/WH/**

www.mwis.org.uk/scottish-forecast/SH/